Have you got everything, Colin?

Alison Hawes
Illustrated by Jacqueline East

RIGBY

"Have you got your school things?" asked Dad.
"I've got my book," said Colin.

"Have you got your lunch box?" asked Dad. "Yes," said Colin.

Dad asked, "Have you got your milk money?" "Yes," said Colin.

"Have you got your
gym shoes?" asked Dad.
"Yes," said Colin.

9

"And I've got my
pencil case," said Colin.
"Good," said Dad.

"Have you got everything?"
asked Dad.
"Yes I have," said Colin.

14